Words of Inspiration

WORDS
OF
INSPIRATION

by John E. Harrison

John E. Harrison

Words of Inspiration

Copyright © 2011
by John E. Harrison 24510-HARR
ISBN: Softcover 978-0-578-09129-7

All rights reserved. No part of this book may be reproduced or transmitted in any form by any means, electronic or mechanical, including photocopying, recording, or by any information storage or retrieval system, without permission in writing from the Publisher.

This book was printed in the United States of America

To order additional copies of this book, contact:
Unique Euphony Publishing Group
706-577-3197

www.uniqueeuphony.com

inquiries@uniqueeuphony.com

Edited by Barbara M. Pierce
Cover Design by Kirk Knox
Photography by Latavia Pierce-Williams

Dedication

This book is dedicated to Regina (Faye) Paschal, who for the past thirteen years, has served in many critical roles of ministry at House of Prayer Christian Church. As church secretary she was always the first to see my writings and was always so gracious with encouragement while silently correcting grammar, Spelling, and punctuation. She has been a constant and dependable confidant who carries many of my personal burdens in her heart. She was never afraid to chastise me for my unwillingness to accept gifts from others as expressions of their love and appreciation for the service I provided. She has always made herself available to serve with willingness and diligence making it easy for me to be so flawed in so many areas of my life yet feels so special.

You were created to see me through some of life's most difficult and challenging moments and you

Words of Inspiration

have and continue to do that with an excellent spirit. I thank you, and I thank God for you.

John E. Harrison
Pastor, HOPCC

Acknowledgements

A huge note of thanks, and appreciation, to the many individuals who have supported the vision of House of Prayer Ministries, during the past thirteen years. A special note of appreciation to Kathy, at Allegra Printing, for retyping and protecting these writings, and for providing copies that made the conversion into book format less tedious.

Tremendous credit is given to Unique Euphony, for risking reputation to publish a book written by an unknown author, whose works remain untested. Thank you for the willingness to take me beyond my dreams.

I am also grateful for all of my friends at the House of Prayer. Your encouragement while listening each Sunday, with convincing enthusiasm, to "The Words of Inspiration" was a huge inspiration in my life. Your shared and expressed interest has encouraged me to continue pursuing a course I am not particularly gifted in.

My wife has also shared the joy of this journey, supported by a loving and caring church family, and has made the demands of ministry much easier. Knowing that the congregation was always there for her, when my energy and efforts were directed

Words of Inspiration

toward the support of others, was a truly wonderful gift.

To those whose lives I have watched in silence, as you went about your days just being yourselves. Co-workers, friends, acquaintances, enemies, pastors, family members, church members, adults, children, professionals, laborers, the caring and the uncaring, the faithful and the unfaithful, the hurting, the healed, the strong, the weak, the healthy, the dying, the lost, and the saved - this book was inspired by you. Thank you for allowing me to see life as it is, and the hope of what it can be, through faith and perseverance.

Thank you to everyone who refuses to allow life to defeat promises, who demand a rematch with every failed endeavor, who see light in scenes of total darkness, and who make the declarations of victory at the beginning and not the end of every day. It is you who have encourage me to write these words of inspiration.

Thanks to all of you!

Thank you,

John E. Harrison

Words of Inspiration

CONTENTS

2008

WE ARE FAMILY   1
THE COST OF CHEAP TALK   2
GALLY'S STORY   3
ALWAYS THANKFUL   4
BEEN THERE DONE THAT   5
WATCH YOUR STEP…SOMEONE IS-   6
FOLLOWING YOU
NOW CHOOSE   8
WHERE IS THE LOVE   9
JUST WAIT AND SEE   10
I DID NOTHING   11
THEY WALKED AWAY   12
FAMILIAR DECEPTION   13
IT HURTS   14
NOW HIRING   16
I NEED TO TALK   17
WE NEED TO TALK   18
A MESSAGE WITHOUT MEANING   19
DON'T QUIT   20
DIAGNOIS MYSTERIOUS   21
THANKS UNTIL YOU ARE BETTER PAID   22
A COMMON REALITY…BUT   23
MY SUFFERING YOUR BENEFIT   24
KNOWING   25
KNOWING HIS PRESENCE AND POWER   26
ENOUGH IS ENOUGH   27
YOUR LIFE IS YOUR WITNESS   28
GOOD DEEDS ABORTED   29
WHAT A DIFFERENCE A DAY MAKES   31

John E. Harrison

Words of Inspiration

LOVE WILL FIND A WAY   32
KEEP TRYING   33
ISSUES UNADDRESSED   34
BEFORE REASON, FORGIVE   35
THINK   36
BUILDING RELATIONSHIPS TOGETHER   37
CONSTANT VERSUS SEASONAL   38
A BODY EXPERENCE   39

2009

INTERRUPTION OR OPPORTUNITY   40
MULTI-TASKING   41
MY PAIN IS MY CUE   42
INSPIRED BY SELF AWARENESS   43
DO YOUR BEST   44
LOVE THAT YOU CAN FEEL   45
A PRAYER OF SUBMISSION TO GOD'S…   46
HE ANSWERED NOT A WORD   47
CONSIDER YOUR WAYS   49
A FATHER EXPECTATION   50
ORDER MY STEPS   51
LET GO AND IT WILL GO   52
THE DOCTOR IS NOT ALWAYS RIGHT   53
YOUR FUTURE IS CERTAIN   54
GRAMMA-KEEP YOUR HANDS ON ME   55
SPEAKING HIS WONDERS IN THE…   56
MAN'S PERSPECTIVE VS GOD'S…   57
HIS ALL SUFFICIENT SUSTAINING …   58
TELL GOD ABOUT IT   59
THE HILLS HAS EYES   60
I PRAYED   61
HE WAS THERE ALL THE TIME   62

IT IS A PREREQUISITE   63
NEVER ALONE   64
AREN'T YOU GLAD YOU BELIEVE IN…   65
OUR ENEMY…OUR BROTHER   66
TRUTH OUT OF TRIVIA   67
STAY FOCUSED…STAY THE COURSE   68
JUDGEMENT WITHHELD DUE   69
A SAD REALITY   70
DOING OUR OWN THIN   71
THAT'S LIFE   72
ARE YOU OK WITH THAT   73
FUNCTIONAL WRECKS   74
I DON'T THINK SO   75
LEADERS FRUSTRATION   76
WHAT IF   78
IT DEPENDS ON THE CIRCUMSTANCES   79
GOD'S LOVE REMAINS CONSTANT   80
A PRAYER OF SURRENDERED WILL   81
IN MOMENTS LIKE THESE   82
HELP ME HOLY GHOST!   83
CONFESS YOUR SINS   84
LEGACY VERSUS FAULTS   85
IT'S A MATTER OF CHOICE   86
MY CONSTANT THOUGHT   87
IT'S NOT OVER UNTIL YOU QUIT   88
REAFFIRM YOUR LOVE DAILY   89
AN OPPORTUNITY TO FORGIVE   90

2010

OUR JOY, OUR BURDEN   91
MY GOAL, MY ENEMY,   92
SUCCEEDING BY DOING NOTHING   93

Words of Inspiration

I SHOULD HAVE PRAYED FOR THE … 94
ISSUES OF THE HEART   95
COMPASSION FATIGUE   96
NOTHING TO SPEAK ABOUT   98
OTHER THAN THAT, IT WAS FINE   100
HE ALWAYS GIVES… 101
HE WILL SUPPLY   102
THANK YOU   103
COUNT YOUR BLESSINGS   104
NO SUBSTITUTE   105
IS THE PROBLEM WORTH … 106
HIS REFLECTION   107
DARK SPOTS IN THE HEART   108
HE HEARS YOU   109
GOD ALWAYS KEEP HIS WORD   110
PLAY LIKE IT…AND DO IT   111
EXPRESS YOURSELF   112
I PLAY CHICKEN AND HIDE   113
WHATCHA LOOKING AT   114
THAT WAS SO LOVE   115
HE GAVE MORE   116
I'LL GET BACK WITH YOU   117
WHEN STUFF HAPPENS   118
WHERE DID THAT COME FROM?   120
YOUR HARVEST IS IN YOUR SEED   121
IT'S GOOD TO KNOW JESUS   122
YOU CAN HANDLE IT   123
THE WORD IS YOUR VICTORY   124
PROMISE KEEPERS, COVENANT… 125
ONE THINGS THOU LACKETH   126
THAT SOUNDS SO LIKE CHRIST   127
DARKNESS IS AS LIGHT TO HIM   128

John E. Harrison

Words of Inspiration

ACCEPT NO GIFTS FROM THE DEVIL   129
JOY AT DAY BREAK   130
IN MOMENTS LIKE THESE   131
BRIDGES OR WALLS   132
I AM TRYING   133
THINK   135
SOMETIMES   136
BECAUSE I SAID I DO   138
THAT BOTHERS ME   140
SOW AND WAIT   142
THE POWER OF LISTENING   143
CAN I TRUST YOU?   145

2011

THE NORMAL CHRISTIAN LIFE   146
MY MORTALITY, HIS PURPOSE   147
HIS WONDERS   148
WHEN I AM WEAK   149
THINKING VERSUS DOING   150
I DEVELOPED INTO MY THOUGHTS   152
YOUR UNIQUENESS CHALLENGED MY   153
PRAISE KEEPS YOU FOCUSED   154
MAKING THINGS HAPPEN   155
DISCIPLINE VERSUS DESTRUCTION   156
NOW THAT I THINK ABOUT IT…   157
I WANTED TO DO BETTER SO I DID   158
I WOULD GIVE ANYTHING   159
DON'T DO IT   160
MY TEARS ARE FOR ME   161
TALK TO ME…I WON'T TELL   162
YOUR SECOND THOUGHT   163
IF I HAD IT TO DO ALL OVER AGAIN   164
ASSAULT ON TRUTH   166

John E. Harrison

- I TRIED HARDER   167
- GOD HATES THAT   168
- WAIT THREE DAYS   169
- REMOVE THE PEBBLES   171
- WEAKNESS SHROUDED BY …   173
- PROFILE OF A GODLY HUSBAND   174
- I CAN'T LET'EM SEE ME LIKE THIS   175
- A LOVE THAT CARES   176
- THE CONSISTENCY OF DESIRE…   177
- BEGGING VERSUS BELIEVING   179
- TRUST HIS LOVE   181
- YOUR VISION IS YOUR BLUEPRINT   183
- ABOUT THE AUTHOR   185

Words of Inspiration

WE ARE FAMILY

To speak with dishonor and disrespect

about any person within the kingdom of God,

is to dishonor and Disrespect every person within his kingdom.

To entertain the dishonorable and or disrespectful

Communications of anyone that is directed toward

any person within God's kingdom is to become an ally of your

own assailant. Please WATCH YOUR MOUTH

when you are talking about my family.

January 6, 2008

John E. Harrison

Words of Inspiration

The Cost of Cheap Talk

The common belief is that talk is cheap
but the real truth is that cheap talk can be extremely costly.
A malicious rumor can cost someone their job,
a lie spoken as a joke can cost someone their reputation,
a loosely spoken statement about a loved one can cost someone
many nights of restless slumber.
Talk is not cheap, cheap talk can be and often is extremely costly.
Therefore if you choose to be a talker it is your responsibility
to insure that what you are saying is worth saying.

January 13, 2008

John E. Harrison

Words of Inspiration

GALLY'S STORY

I had the distinct honor of sitting in the presence of a person who has lived for one hundred plus years. She revealed unwaveringly that her present and daily goal is "to live the life so I can die the death." She summed up her life's journey looking over her right shoulder raising her frail, shriveled right arm with a determined commitment pointing toward the west. She pulled into perspective to whole of her life with all of its ventures and adventures. The words that followed are what I like to refer to as "Gally's Story." She said, "I started out not too far down yonder and one hundred years later I am not far from where I started." Gally's Story is obviously about her natural life's journey from her natural birth to her present experience. Could Gally's story reflect the spiritual journey of many of us who are gathered here today? From your new birth experience until now has your journey been one of considerable progress or can you say as did Gally, pointing back to your new birth experience. "I am not very far from where I started out."

January 20, 2008

John E. Harrison

Words of Inspiration

ALWAYS THANKFUL

My grand-daughter Jayne was introduced to the use of the cell phone by her grandmother who taught her to always call and thank me for the allowance that I gave her twice each month. The script would go as follows; Helen would dial the number to my cell phone, and pass the phone to Jayne informing her that papa was on the phone instructing her in this manner, "Tell papa thank you for my allowance," and so she would. Because of this seemingly simple practice of expressing gratitude for gifts given on a consistent basis, whenever Jayne communicates with me by cell phone she always begins her conversation with the greeting "Ha papa" immediately followed by "thank you for my allowance," Jayne is always thankful.

How do you approach God your father, who has been far more gracious in the things he has provided for you with a far greater degree of dependability?

Are you always asking or are you like my granddaughter Jayne, always thankful?

January 2, 2008

John E. Harrison

Words of Inspiration

BEEN THERE DONE THAT

The obstacles that you have overcome in the past ought to serve as a source of hope for victories in the future. Therefore your faith should never be shaken by your present circumstances but shaped and sharpened by your past conquests, as a result, as you are confronted by the unfolding of life's challenges you too will be able to affirm, as did the psalmist with faith undaunted,

"I've been there, and I've done that."

February 11, 2008

Words of Inspiration

WATCH YOUR STEP…

SOMEONE IS FOLLOWING YOU

As I sat in McDonald's one Saturday morning eating a pancake breakfast as it is my custom to do on occasions when I am left alone to provide for myself, or when I am up early due a requirement to fulfill work obligations; the atmosphere was anything but pleasant. The noise of retirees telling war stories reminded me of unpleasant events in my life that I would have preferred left undisturbed. The pancakes and the syrup were cold and I questioned the sane reasoning of anyone who would choose to spend even the smallest amount of hard earned money in such a place.

Just as I was about to push my food aside, and declare my attempt to cheat and treat myself to some forbidden food, a complete failure, a young well groomed man and a much younger male child entered the building, and walked up to the counter and with deliberation precision, placed an order, and was given their food and they immediately exited the building without conversation or delay. As they moved toward the door with the child following the adult I was intrigued by the child's attempt to stretch his stride in order to walk in the footsteps of his adult leader.

John E. Harrison

Never once did the adult look back therefore was not aware of the fact that the path that he was taking was directly influencing the course of his younger companion. In that moment a voice from within me spoke this warning to all who would walk recklessly before the young and impressionable. "WATCH YOUR STEP… SOMEONE IS FOLLOWING YOU."

February 17, 2008

Words of Inspiration

NOW CHOOSE

Everywhere I look there is published bold statement

that encourages the shaking off of all of the restraints

that would suggest a life lived on a higher moral plain.

Nike says, "Just Do It." Burger King says," Have It Your Way."

One old school song writer said,

"It's Your Thing Do What You Want to Do."

But before you choose there is another saying

that you should consider, "proverbs 3:5-6 says

"Trust in the Lord with all Thine Heart;

and Lean not unto Thine Own Understanding.

In all thy ways acknowledge him,

and he shall direct Thy Path." Now Choose!

February 24, 2008

John E. Harrison

Words of Inspiration

WHERE IS THE LOVE?

The credibility of the witness of the church is directly linked to the unity of its members. If there is to be an authentic example of the God kind of love for the world to witness the church has been given that Responsibility. If there is to be a direction in which a lost and groping world may look with an optimist up-look it must be to the church. What the world needs now is living demonstration of love not another sermon preached about love: It needs to see love not hear about love; It needs to see love's action not hear about love's potential. The witness of the world against the church often sounds like this, "I see the church, the building, the steeple and the multitudes of people but what I don't see is the love."

Since I am here
so as not to have wasted a trip
would someone be so kind as to show me where the
love hangs out in this church.

March 2, 2008

Words of Inspiration

JUST WAIT AND SEE

I was inspired by a scene from an episode of walker, Texas Ranger. A friend of a former ranger, CD Parker's son had been wounded in a shootout whose life depended on him receiving blood to replace that which he had lost as a result of his injury. CD's blood type just happens to be a match and he gladly donated the blood that would save the young man's life, and after the medical procedure was over, CD slowly pushing his shirt sleeve down reassured the wounded boy's father by saying, "everything's going to be alright Hank, just you wait and see." What an assurance it is to know that once the blood of Jesus has been applied to whatever situation you are facing in your own personal struggles in life, the only challenge remaining is that you just wait and see.

March 16, 2008

Words of Inspiration

I DID NOTHING

What would you say to someone from within this congregation
who you knew was being physically, verbally, and emotionally abused?

What would you do if you knew of someone from within this congregation
who was being held hostage by fear and depleted self-will in a prison
called home by an abusive mate?

Would you go to them with words of encouragement
and declaration of love and support or would you
say as do so many
(so called caring church folk)
"I didn't know what to do, so I did nothing"

March 23, 2008

John E. Harrison

Words of Inspiration

THEY WALKED AWAY

An agency that specialized in protecting women who were being victimized by abusive mates received a call from a frightened, physically bruised, emotionally shattered woman who whispered an unmistakably desperate plea, "I need your help." When the woman met with owner/representative of the protection agency and began to explain the details of her abusive relationship with her mate she quickly realized that he was without even a vague understanding of the bondage into which she was being held nor the abuse that she was forced to endure, and with that she walked away. How many broken, helpless, battered members of the human family have responded to the message of hope that echoes from the pulpits of churches not unlike the one in which we are now seated only to realize that even though our message is one of hope we are often without the vaguest understanding of the depth of hopelessness that has become their present reality, and with that, "They have walked away."

March 30, 2008

John E. Harrison

Words of Inspiration

FAMILIAR DECEPTION

Sometimes it is easier to be deceived by

someone with whom we share things in common

than by

those with whom our differences are obvious.

Don't be fooled by the familiar.

April 6, 2008

Words of Inspiration

IT HURTS

When your baby cries all night and the atmosphere of your place of employment is both demanding and insensitive.

When the child that you have given diligence to bring up in the fear of the lord
chooses a life course that defies all that he or she has been taught to respect.

When it becomes your duty to explain to your children
that the unit that once represented a family is now broken.

When you can no longer explain away the scares of the abuse
that has been consistent with what you have convinced
yourself to be normal and therefore acceptable to endure for the sake of the children.

When something inside of you rises up and declares
…No more!
And

John E. Harrison

Words of Inspiration

when in that moment of your declared freedom you discover
that there is no one there to love you.

It Hurts.

April 13, 2008

John E. Harrison

Words of Inspiration

NOW HIRING

Someone who is interested in participating in a promising life that is yet unfolding. Someone who is willing to work overtime and is available for both day and night shifts. Someone who is flexible and is on call twenty four hours a day seven days a week.

Must be willing to work holidays and weekends

Must be a good listener

Godly counselor

with a respect for confidentiality

position title: "A friend"

April 20, 2008

Words of Inspiration

I NEED TO TALK

Have you ever woke up in the middle of the night

with a need to talk to someone?

But who do you call at that hour

that would not make it obvious that

you have called at a really bad time?

Imagine the response: Do you know what time it is?

Yeah, its mid-night, but I still need to talk.

April 27, 2008

Words of Inspiration

We Need To Talk

Reconciliation begins with communication. As long as you remain silent in your differences you will also remain separate in your endeavors. Communication is the one essential ingredient in establishing, building, maintaining, repairing and restoring a healthy relationship. So, if there is a breach in your relationship that has robbed you of your oneness as married couples or dear, dear friends, reparation begins with a simple declaration,

"We Need to Talk."

May 4, 2008

Words of Inspiration

Message without Meaning

I was watching a scene in an episode of Gun smoke, where three young troubled teens who had been placed on probation under the supervision of a devout old preacher, were being lectured on the law of seed time and harvest, when the lecture was finally over As the fiery old preacher walked away, one of the young men, shaking his head with an expression of angry intolerance, confessed unashamedly, "I am getting fed up with that old man's preaching." To that comment, one of the young man's companions in crime, in an attempt to comfort him, offered these words, "Don't pay him no mind Vergil, He didn't mean anything by it." Fortunately that statement was not true of the Dodge City preacher, but many who stand in pulpits all over the world are indeed, preaching a message that they themselves, "Really Do Not Mean."

May 11, 2008

Words of Inspiration

Don't Quit

Quitting always results in your living in the shadow of what you could have been. With your final thoughts being, what if I had...I wonder where I would be if I had...If only...I should've...The only acceptable stopping point for you is at the outer borders of your own potential.

Your potential is your only referee. And he always speaks from within you. He will also be the final voice to evaluate your life's achievements. Not on the basis of how well you have done the things you have attempted, but on the basis of how true you have been to developing into your true self.

Therefore if you are not a resident of the outer border of your potential, listen to the voice within you, a voice that will not be silenced by intermediate success and press on. I know you are tired, but please for the sake of your own peace in your final moments of life, **"Don't Quit!"**

July 20, 2008

John E. Harrison

Words of Inspiration

Diagnosis Mysterious

When illnesses come we look to doctors to give us answers, but what if they can't? In these instances diagnosis becomes a mystery. But to God the mystery is known. Through Him it shall be revealed and by the precious blood of Jesus He promises that it shall be healed

July 27, 2008

Words of Inspiration

THANKS, UNTIL YOU ARE BETTER PAID

There is a day coming when all of your labors will be judged and due compensations distributed in the form of rewards for the deeds you have done. Therefore, the intermediate expression of gratitude that flows from the lips of men seems so insignificant in the light of that which is to come.

To those of you, who have labored and do continue to labor, do not grow weary in your well doing. Your day of recognition has been scheduled and it shall come. But, in the meantime let me just say, "THANKS, until you are better paid."

August 3, 2008

John E. Harrison

Words of Inspiration

A COMMON REALITY, BUT…

A recent hospital visit positioned me by the bedside of a middle aged African American male, (a terminal cancer patient) who suffered extreme physical pain and emotional anguish as he reconciles within himself, the reality of his own mortality. He said, with a deep sigh, slumping over the serving table upon which sat the evening meal that he had neither the desire nor the energy to consume, "I guess I just have to live with the fact that I am dying."

As he pondered things undone, people unseen, grandchildren not yet held, family, kin, siblings, sons and daughters…Yet, after A long pause of the deepest silence his conclusion was, "I am dying and I have nowhere to go."

As I considered the reality of my patient's distastefully bitter end to a brief span of the time spent here in this earthly realm, his fate whispered, "death is a reality that is common to us all, however our destination after death is a matter of individual choice."

Death is a common reality, the question is…will life, eternal life be a reality after your death?

August 10, 2008

John E. Harrison

Words of Inspiration

MY SUFFERING, YOUR BENEFIT

What I have learned in and through my past struggles have equipped me with the experiential insight needed to help you survive with victory in your present dilemma.

It really is good for you that I have suffered that I would learn to minister more effectively to you in your time of affliction.

                    August 17, 2008

KNOWING

Trust in God is knowing while in your struggles, even as you deal with your natural tendency to doubt, fear, give in or even quit…That God will bring your prevailing problem to a positive end. Therefore, while you may have cause to question or doubt many things, never, ever doubt or question your knowing.

August 24, 2008

Words of Inspiration

KNOWING HIS PRESENCE AND POWER

WHILE IT IS DIFFICULT TO WATCH ANY OF YOU SUFFER…IF I COULD TAKE AWAY YOUR PAIN, REMOVE ALL OF YOUR OBSTACLES AND DESTROY YOUR LAST ENEMY, I WOULD NOT. BECAUSE IN DOING SO IT WOULD DENY YOU THE PRIVILEGE OF EVER KNOWING, AS I KNOW, THE PRESENCE AND POWER OF GOD IN YOUR BEST AND WORST OF TIMES.

August 31, 2008

John E. Harrison

Enough Is Not Enough

"Enough is enough" is a statement that often flows out from or in response to the demands made by the issues of life that offers nothing in response to your constant giving. Enough in this context, limits proportions, it issues a portion out from the whole. Enough holds back something for more personal uses, it reserves for the unforeseen.

Enough from a spiritual perspective denies God access to all that He requires of you. From that perspective, it is my conclusion that enough is not enough, therefore, until you have given ALL that God requires of you, until you have done ALL that He requires that you should do, though you may have given and done much, still you simply have not given or done enough.

Therefore, if your enough is not your ALL…Your enough is not enough.

SORRY…

September 7, 2008

Words of Inspiration

YOUR LIFE IS YOUR WITNESS

A LINE FROM THE MOVIE "THE GLADIATOR" ARRESTED MY ATTENTION AND SET ME TO PONDING A SERIOUS REALITY. IT WENT LIKE THIS, "WHAT WE DO IN LIFE ECHOES IN ETERNITY." THE QUESTION THAT FLOWS OUT OF THIS REALITY IS, "ARE YOU PREPARED TO BE CONFRONTED WITH THE LIFE YOU HAVE LIVED WHEN YOU STAND BEFORE THE JUDGEMENT SEAT OF CHRIST?" WILL YOUR LIFE BE A WITNESS FOR YOU OR AGAINST YOU?

September 14, 2008

John E. Harrison

Words of Inspiration

Good Deeds Aborted

Have you ever thought about performing a positive act for the benefit of someone for no reason other than "Just because" and before you could initiate that high and noble deed you talked yourself out of going through with it?

I thought about calling a friend who I had not spoke to for some time but it was after nine pm, so I didn't.

I thought about calling that family who is without transportation to see if they needed a ride to the grocery store to pick up items for Sunday dinner, but I reasoned that if they needed a ride they would call me, so I didn't.

I thought about slipping a crumpled up twenty dollar bill into the hand of a fellow church member who I knew was experiencing financial difficulty but I remembered that Wal-Mart was having a sale on flavored bottled water, so I spent it there instead.

I thought about offering a ride to a mother and her children one Saturday afternoon as I watched them leaving Piggly Wiggly on foot, as it slowly began to drizzle, but I reasoned that they were accustomed to walking and to interfere would only interrupt their cycle of normalcy, so I didn't.

Thoughts give birth to deeds. Positive thoughts that fail to produce positive deeds are in essence 'GOOD DEEDS ABORTED."

September 21, 2008

Words of Inspiration

WHAT A DIFFERENCE A DAY MAKES

Mandi Abair, a jazz artists' debut album released in 2000, entitled "Always And Never The Same," is loaded with insight into the ever changing life of one who is under the constant growth and spiritually upgrading ministry of the Holy Spirit. It suggest that if your life is not always different, always evolving, if your life is not made unpredictably different with each passing day…It could be that you have not surrendered to the constant growth and upgrading ministry of the Holy Spirit.

Words of Inspiration

LOVE WILL FIND A WAY

The implication of the above title is that there is no challenge that we could possibly face in life that love, if given the Opportunity, cannot overcome.

No dispute that love cannot reconcile. No broken relationship that love cannot restore. No bruised or broken heart that love cannot heal. No sin against you or God that love cannot forgive.

Therefore if you are faced with a situation in your life that is proving to be too difficult for you to handle, and all of your efforts toward resolution have failed, and you just don't know what to do. May I offer just one suggestion? Let LOVE take a look at it. And I bet you a dollar to a doughnut…LOVE WILL FIND A WAY!

October 5, 2008

Words of Inspiration

KEEP TRYING

I can remember watching my grandson Fabian, while attempting to complete homework assignments learning to form letters as he would become frustrated because he was unable to make the letters he was writing on the paper look more like the picture of the letters he had formed in his mind. In frustration he would crumple up his paper tossing it to the floor declaring in sheer disgust, "I keep messing up," often refusing to continue.

Now that Fabian has gotten older he has learned not only to make his letters on paper look more like the ones he has envisioned in his mind, he has also learned that messing up is not a cue to quit but to "KEEP TRYING."

Perhaps you like Fabian have found yourself in the same kind of seemingly hopeless situation unable to make your life in reality look more like the life God has ordained that you should live and the temptation is to throw in the towel. I understand your frustration, but before you give up on yourself ask Fabian for his opinion of your situation and I am convinced that his advice would be "Don't You Dare Quit, Get Back In There and KEEP TRYING!"

October 12, 2008

Words of Inspiration

Issues Unaddressed

While you masquerade in your homespun garment of self acclaimed perfection, there exists the real possibility that, you've got issues. Issues that no one will dare address because to address them might disrupt that which you contribute to a particular process, program, relationship or ministry.

Will spend time with you. Go out with you and yes, have sex with you. But!!! Will never marry you.

Why? Because you've got issues.

While you are thinking you've got it going on. They are thinking

(But will never say) "You've got problems."

Issues unaddressed cause's people to believe that they are alright when in reality they are not. They are simply being used by a circle of folk who pretend to care.

October 19, 2008

John E. Harrison

Words of Inspiration

BEFORE REASON, FORGIVE

When you feel as though you have been wronged and the pain of it brings you to bitter tears; and an overwhelming need to verbalize the smorgasbord of emotions that are welling up inside beckons you to the table of negotiation with your wrongdoer, consider this as your agenda.

Before attempting to reason with the one who has done you wrong, forgive the wrong that has been done.

October 26, 2008

Words of Inspiration

THINK

The one major contributor to the disruption of harmony between those who are engaged in building healthy relationships is…making hasty comments that have not been censored by the wisdom of the word nor approved by the spirit of God. So if you find yourself with blanket and pillow in hand spending frequent nights in the front room, or living what should be your happiest days engaged in a cold war in that place that should represent a bit of heaven on earth as a result of your thoughtless verbiage and you really would like for the cycle to end. The answer is so simple a caveman can do it.

Think before you speak

November 2, 2008

Words of Inspiration

BUILDING RELATIONSHIPS TOGETHER

If you have not made some sacrificial contributions to the building and maintaining of healthy relationships with the significant people in your life….you are a taker…not a giver. Chances are you're more tolerated based upon the love that others have for you rather than appreciated for the contributions you have made for them.

November 9, 2008

Words of Inspiration

CONSTANT VERSUS SEASONAL

The season that is rapidly gathering upon us has traditionally become a season of liberality and caring; joy and celebration; peace and goodwill. It is also customary that when this season has passed, along with it passes the attitude for which this season has become known.

The bible teaches that giving and caring ought not to be stimulated by seasons it should be motivated by the obvious and eternal presence of human needs.

The bible also teaches that there will always be a presence of needs represented by the conditions of the impoverished with which we are privileged to coexist. Privileged because the constant presence of the needs of others, represent constant opportunities for us to demonstrate God's love and concern for members of the human family.

CARING SHOULD BE CONSTANT NOT SEASONAL!

November 23, 2008

John E. Harrison

Words of Inspiration

A BODY EXPERIENCE

THE HUMAN BODY IS CREATED IN SUCH A MANNER THAT WHATEVER ANY PART OF THE BODY FEELS, IT IS FELT THROUGHOUT THE BODY. BECAUSE OF THIS UNIQUE WIRING SYSTEM WITHIN THE BODY IT IS NOT POSSIBLE FOR PAIN OR TRAUMA, MINUTE OR SEVERE, TO INVADE ANY PART OF THE BODY IN INCIDENTS OF ISOLATION.

THE CHURCH IS ALSO REFERRED TO AS A BODY, <u>THE BODY OF CHRIST</u>. LIKE THE HUMAN BODY, BECAUSE OF ITS UNIQUE CONNECTION BY THE SPIRIT OF CHRIST, IT IS NOT POSSIBLE FOR PAIN OR TRAUMA, MINUTE OR SEVERE TO BE THE EXPERIENCE OF ONE WITHOUT IT ENEVITABLY BECOMING

<u>A BODY EXPERIENCE.</u>

December 21, 2008

John E. Harrison

Words of Inspiration

INTERRUPTION or OPPORTUNITY

As I sat at my computer desk working vigorously to complete an assigned task in order to be prepared for a critical inspection that will take place in a few days. A newly hired employee entered my work space requesting my assistance in loading two rather heavy boxes into her vehicle to transport to her home for sorting and filing.

The very first fleeting thought that crossed my mind was I really don't have time for this. I have my own deadline to meet and I really don't need this interruption.

As I walked away after having placed the last of the materials onto the backseat of her car insuring that the files would not move as she drove to her Harris County residence. A voice within my conscience (The Holy Spirit) retorted. Was that really an <u>interruption</u> to the completion of your task or was it an <u>opportunity</u> to help someone else accomplish theirs?

January 4, 2009

John E. Harrison

Words of Inspiration

MULTI-TASKING

One of the buzz words that identify the movers and shakers of the cooperate community is multi-tasking.

Multi-Tasking speaks of one's ability to successfully focus on and accomplish more than one task at a time. It highlights one's ability to think simultaneously in multiple directions

Multi- tasking in the corporate community simply defined is the ability to do at least two things at the same time.

However, multi-tasking in the Christian community is the ability to handle your own affairs while at the same time helping someone else in their time of needs.

Therefore, if you are ever confronted with a plea for help at a time when you are deeply involved with the management of your own affairs that would be a perfect opportunity for you to demonstrate your ability to think in two directions.

<u>A PERFECT OPPORTUNITY FOR MULTI-TASKING</u>

January 11, 2009

John E. Harrison

Words of Inspiration

My Pain is my Cue

When I find myself experiencing the pain that is consistent with life lived under the rule of suffering and uncertainty, I am immediately reminded that struggling is not unique to me alone; there are countless others whose life experiences are far worse than mine. So instead of focusing on my own pain or drowning in my own sorrow. My pain is my cue to become a burden bearer for someone else.

January 18, 2009

John E. Harrison

Inspired by Self Awareness

If there is ever a time when you are not sure how to help someone in their time of need, first think of what you would do for yourself if you had the same need and simply…do that.

January 25, 2009

Words of Inspiration

DO YOUR BEST

When you have done your best to faithfully fulfill the task that God has called you to, and your constant reminder by those around you is of how miserably you have failed. You are provided with one of two options; you can allow yourself to become so overwhelmed by the surrounding negativity and just quit, or you can simply continue to do your best.

February 1, 2009

Words of Inspiration

LOVE THAT YOU CAN FEEL

What is your attitude toward the poor, the needy, those who are always in need of help or support of some kind? Is it that of intolerance, disgust, indifference or down-right hostility? But wait! Before you respond, allow me to remind you that these are the ones that Jesus said will always provide you with opportunities to be a tangible expression of his love.

February 8, 2009

Words of Inspiration

A PRAYER OF SUBMISSION TO GOD'S WORD IN THE MIDST OF A TRIAL

"Lord I need your strength infused in me, and I submit to the truth of your word. My responses, attitudes, actions, and thoughts are all in submission to your word. Amen"

February 12, 2009

Words of Inspiration

HE ANSWERED NOT A WORD

Doc Adams of the western Gun Smoke had been tending a young couple who were expecting their first child. As the time for delivery drew near doc was summoned to the young couple's home to assist with delivery, but as he was leaving his Dodge City office, he witnessed a robbery/murder with the murderer left wounded lying in the street. Doc immediately decided to remain in town to provide help to the wounded murderer sending a mid-wife to assist the young couple with delivery of their baby; a decision that resulted in the death of the child.

When the father of the deceased baby realized that Doc had chosen to save a murderer's life, instead of responding to the needs of his wife, he was furious. Attacking Doc Adams, he pushed him with such force that it sent Doc hurling backward landing in a Garbage heap. At the same time he was hurling evil accusations, "you old quack it is your fault that my baby died…You old fool!"

John E. Harrison

Doc could have explained the Hippocratic Oath. He could have reasoned about his hopes to save both the baby and the murderer, but he didn't. He lowered his head, and questioning his own judgment with his shoulders drooped. He dragged himself up the stairs to his humble office abode…

<u>Answering him not a word.</u>

How like Christ, Doc's response was.

February 15, 2009

Words of Inspiration

CONSIDER YOUR WAYS

It is becoming a common practice for those who profess faith in God, validated by a new birth experience. To approach life applying the same basic principles, moral values, exhibiting the same basic characteristics in daily living, as the world. This approach to life as Christians seems to indicate a belief that the manner in which we have lived here on earth will be forever forgotten at life's end. However, scripture reveals that at the judgment seat of Christ the manner in which we have lived will be viewed under divine scrutiny and rewards issued or forfeited on the basic of the deeds we've done in the body. With that thought in mind, wisdom would suggest, "<u>Consider your ways</u> if you are not to be ashamed at that time when Christ examines your works."

February 22, 2009

John E. Harrison

Words of Inspiration

A FATHER'S EXPECTATION

As a proud father updated me on the athletic activities of his son, he boasted of his ability to excel in both football and basketball. This father's future prospects for his son were obviously hopeful with an optimistic outlook. In that the father provided a genetic foundation for his son to grow in physical statue to a proportion that would be consistent with his athletic potential.

The father said with unwavering confidence "He's going to be tall because I am tall. Look at me I'm 6' 4'', weighing two hundred plus pounds." This statement strongly implies that because of the father's physical statue his expectation is that his son will eventually develop and grow into his likeness.

With that thought in mind…

Imagine what God, our heavenly father's expectation of his children must be.

March 1, 2009

John E. Harrison

Words of Inspiration

ORDER MY STEPS

Waiting challenges man's natural tendency to manage his own affairs…to be independent rather than dependent. Yet life presents many situations that are not accompanied by the needed resources, wisdom or opportunity to effectively resolve the things that confront us in order that we may move on with life experiencing minimal delay.

So we find ourselves waiting.

Waiting for answers.

Waiting for situational changes.

Waiting for breakthroughs.

The temptation is to find our own answers, affect our own changes, and orchestrate our own breakthroughs. But before you yield to that temptation, wisdom would counsel. "Be absolutely certain that the steps you are about to take are ordered by **God.**

March 8, 2009

John E. Harrison

Words of Inspiration

LET GO AND IT WILL GO

Much of the pains of our past that we continue to re-live as a constant present experience is often the result of a daily, self –imposed agony based upon our choice to hold on to those unpleasant experiences through conversation, meditation or unforgiveness; As a result the hurt continues to be as real and as fresh as it was when the wound was initially inflicted. The answer to this problem is simple let go of the past with all of its painful experiences.

<u>If you will let go, it will go away.</u>

March 15, 2009

THE DOCTOR IS NOT ALWAYS RIGHT

I was watching one of my favorite episodes of walker, Texas Ranger, when the show was interrupted by one of many commercials. One of which caught my attention. It went like this: "I was in the grocery store when I had a heart-attack. I took a Bayer Aspirin out of my purse and chewed it. My doctor said the aspirin saved my life."

While we all would like to think that the doctor we have chosen as our primary care giver is always accurate in his diagnosis and treatment. However, in this particular case it proves that the doctor is not always right. Aspirin is neither the giver nor the sustainer of life.

Only God can do that.

March 22, 2009

Words of Inspiration

YOUR FUTURE IS CERTAIN

As I watched an unfamiliar western on my wife Helen's favorite channel. A group of immigrants were confronted with the challenge to defend themselves against ruthless investors determined to force them off their land in order to build a railroad through their property.

As they engaged in the process of brainstorming, searching for their best possible course of action, one of the defenders reflected on the successful methods they had used in similar situations in the past; A reflection that was met with the statement, "The past is always certain."

The implication of this statement is that you can only be certain of the things that have already happened. But a greater more profound truth is this, with God <u>your future is just as certain as your past.</u>

March 29, 2009

John E. Harrison

Words of Inspiration

GRAM-MA-KEEP YOUR HANDS ON ME

As we sat in the kitchen one rainy Saturday morning with Helen preparing breakfast and Jayne sitting in one of the four pub chairs around the kitchen table, Jayne, in her excitement, sipping her coffee and taunting her Papa, slipped and almost fell from her seat.

Realizing the danger a fall from that height presented she made a sudden request of her Granma that was simple and purposeful. First she said to herself in a whisper "I almost fell" them she made her request…it went like this, "Granma, keep your hands on me, so I don't fall."

When you find yourself in a situation that threatens your safely or your stability either physical, emotional or spiritual. Why not cry out to God in prayer, as Jayne cried out to her Granma in fear, "Lord keeps your hand on me, so I don't fall."

April 5, 2009

John E. Harrison

Words of Inspiration

SPEAKING HIS WONDERS IN THE MIDST OF LIFE'S MYSTERIES

(An Excerpt from Doing the Word)

The way we view God…our perception of God can always be identified by the manner in which we speak when we are going through tough times. Our conversation in our times of trouble will always reveal how seriously we have accepted God as he has revealed himself in times past.

If we have seriously taken hold of the self revelation of God, no matter what happens in our lives our conversation will always be hopeful…Our friend will still be Jesus, though our souls be overwhelmed and our bodies bent our boast will always be in the Lord. Our victory will still be in Jesus.

<u>Always speaking the wonders of God even in the midst of the mysteries of life</u>.

April 12, 2009

Words of Inspiration

Man's Perspective vs. God's Reality

My constant prayer is, "Lord Help my perspective to always line up with your reality."

Sometimes the way we see things in our natural sight is not the way they really are in the sight of God. What God has promised is, in fact, an unchangeable reality yet unfolding. Faith causes us to see those things which are yet unfolding as reality…it is faith that causes our perspective to line up with God's reality.

LET US PRAY

"Lord helps our perspective to always line up with your reality in Jesus' name, **AMEN**"

April 19, 2009

John E. Harrison

Words of Inspiration

HIS ALL-SUFFICIENT SUSTAINING GRACE

In the scriptures, Paul wrote about what he referred to as a thorn in the flesh that was a source of constant trouble and perhaps pain in his life. He tells us that in his effort to find relief he engaged in what I like to refer to as, panic prayer. Three times he petitioned God on this matter, but found no relief. Paul's perspective of his situation did not change until he heard God's response to his prayers.

Maybe you have been praying about a situation in your life and have found no relief. Let me be the first to assure you that God heard you when you first prayed… Now allow me to suggest that you find the time to hear his response, and in doing so, you too may be reminded and assured as was the apostle Paul of his <u>all sufficient sustaining grace.</u>

April 26, 2009

Words of Inspiration

TELL GOD ABOUT IT

Worry has made itself an almost inescapable part of life, both for the saved and the unsaved citizens of the human family. It shows up in the form of constant concerns and ponderings about our future. The future of our children, the economy, the well being of our family. Our health, retirement funds dwindling, and the list go on.

Perhaps you have found yourself in a state of persistently pondering things important over which you feel you have no control; before you surrender to the chaos of the mental processing of your mind, allow me to recommend the words recorded in Philippians 4:6 "Be careful for nothing, but in everything by prayer and supplication with thanksgiving let your request be made known unto God"

Therefore, don't panic find something to be thankful for, and as for your concerns.

<u>TELL GOD ABOUT IT</u>

May 5, 2009

Words of Inspiration

THE HILLS HAS EYES

I woke up early Thursday morning pondering many things that demanded my time and attention. What I would preach on Thursday night. Who needed special prayer; how could I meet work deadlines and not be forced to work on Mother's Day.

In all this I declared "I will look to the hills from whence comes my help; my help comes from the Lord." And in that moment I was humbled by the reality that…from the hill to which I now looked. God had been watching over me all night long.

Perhaps you too, sometimes find yourself feeling somewhat overwhelmed by the demands of life… May I suggest that you do as I did? Look to the hills and be comforted in knowing that from those hills God is also watching over you.

May 10, 2009

I PRAYED

I wanted to give a gift that encompassed more than I had in my possession. At first I felt a sense of discouragement, and was tempted to allow myself to be defeated by my circumstance, and then I remembered that passage of scripture that says, "The effectual fervent prayers of a righteous man availeth much." So, instead of giving in or giving up. I offered a gift that keeps on giving.

I PRAYED.

May 17, 2009

Words of Inspiration

HE WAS THERE ALL THE TIME

Have you ever found yourself searching frantically for something that was right there in plain sight or within arm's reach? Your glasses only to realize that they were already on your eyes; your keys to later discover that you were holding them in your hand; your hat that was already warming your head.

In like manner have you ever found yourself waiting for God to show up in a particular situation that you were going through, only to later realize that <u>he was there all the time.</u>

May 24, 2009

IT IS A PREREQUISITE

The bible tells us that before Jesus began his earthly ministry, he was led by the Holy Spirit, into the wilderness to be tempted (tested) by Satan.

Have you ever found yourself questioning where you were because the things you were going through seemed inconsistent with your idea of an appropriate reward for obedience?

The truth of the matter is, your obedience has to be tested, it has to be tried, and it has to be validated. It has to be tempered in the fire of trials that it may be proven, in order that you may be confidently released into your purpose. <u>It's simply a matter of prerequisite.</u>

May 31, 2009

Words of Inspiration

NEVER ALONE

When life presents those moments when you have been abandoned by friends, attacked by enemies, and you feel as though you have been forsaken by God, fight the temptation to trust your feeling and focus on the promise. "I will never leave you nor will I forsake you" And by this, know that you are

<u>Never Alone.</u>

June 7, 2009

Words of Inspiration

AREN'T YOU GLAD YOU BELIEVE IN MIRACLES?

When you have done your best to do your best and all have failed miserably.

When the challenges of life's unfolding prove to be more powerful that your ability to overcome.

When hope for a better tomorrow has been swallowed up by the gapping mouth of despair… and all reasons' counsel would be for you to give up…your case is hopeless …beyond the reach of human intervention.

In times like these

<u>AREN'T YOU GLAD YOU BELIEVE IN MIRACLES?</u>

June 14, 2009

John E. Harrison

Words of Inspiration

OUR ENEMY…OUR BROTHER

As we consider our wealth and or possession, the normal and acceptable way of thinking is to always make our resources available and accessible only to our family and our friends.

But there is another way of thinking that says, if we will make our resource available to God for use in accomplishing his broader purpose, he will in the process. TRANSFORM OUR ENEMY TO OUR BROTHER

HOW BOUT DAT?

JUNE 19, 2009

Words of Inspiration

TRUTH OUT OF TRIVIA

As I sat in my barber shop waiting for my name to be called for my usual high and tight, white wall, brush cut, the question was being debated about the exact time of the rising of the sun each morning. There were several opinions offered on the subject but the one that captured my attention was offered by the shop's owner whose professional name is Doc Hollywood. (Who by the way, is a skilled debater on any subject)

Doc was precise in his answer, boldly and confidently citing the reason for his unwavering certainty. His answer went like this "it came up at 6:22, the reason I know is because it woke me up"

I said "True that" The Son indeed…isn't it amazing how GOD can bring profound truth out of such senseless trivia?

June 28, 2009

John E. Harrison

Words of Inspiration

STAY FOCUSED…STAY THE COURSE

When the demands upon your life are overwhelming and constant. Never allow your focus upon GOD to be interrupted.

I have discovered that if you will stay focused on HIM you will also be able to stay the course that is before you.

July 5, 2009

Words of Inspiration

JUDGEMENT WITHHELD DUE TO INCONCLUSIVE EVIDENCE

Every action has a story behind it that explains and or justifies the decisions made by others, decision that often results in causing pain, disappointment, anxiety, and anguish to undeserving others.

The immediate human reaction to these experiences is too quickly and decisively. You may judge and pass sentences on the perpetrator, however since we are not privy to the story behind the action, wisdom would counsel, and exercise your right of choice to stamp it with the bold seal of your individual authority decreeing:

<u>Judgment withheld due to inconclusive evidence</u>

July 12, 2009

John E. Harrison

Words of Inspiration

A SAD REALITY

One of the frequent yet fleeting concerns of any of GOD's servant leaders is that after they have given all in the service of the people of GOD. Their labor would be under-rated and unappreciated or both.

The Sad truth of this matter is that those concerns more often than not prove to be <u>their reality.</u>

July 19, 2009

DOING OUR OWN THING

Jesus taught his disciples to pray "Thy will be done on earth as it is in heaven" However, the sad reality is, that too often the will of man is exerted over the will of GOD, resulting in the purpose of GOD for that moment being forever lost.

It is heartbreakingly sad to even think of the many opportunities we have missed to be blessed and to be a blessing to the kingdom simply because we insisted on doing our own thing.

July 26, 2009

Words of Inspiration

THAT'S LIFE

Birth and death seems to define the experience of human existence, however between these two significant events are a host of ongoing activities, experiences and or events.

Books are written, dreams realized, falling in love, falling out of trees, broken hearts, broken arms, broken spirits, broken promises, times of prosperity, times of famine, marriage, divorce, disappointments, discouragement, mamas leaving papas, fathers who were never there, failures in school, failures in ministry, discoveries, disasters, distress, cancer, diabetes, hypertension, stroke, decisions made, decisions questioned, trust, distrust, doubt, fear, excitement, disgust, peace, anxiety, wanna stay, compelled to leave, loving, hating, forgiving, blaming, loyalty, cheating, abstinence, promiscuity, mothers awake all night, where is your father when I really need him. Questions, Questions, so many questions.

WHAT IS THIS?

That MY FRIEND…WELL…<u>THAT'S JUST LIFE</u>

August 2, 2009

John E. Harrison

Words of Inspiration

ARE YOU OK WITH THAT?

A TV commercial developed to improve the sale of peanut butter casted a father and his daughter sitting at a breakfast table having a father-daughter conversation while the father prepared a snack for himself and his daughter by spreading peanut butter on an open slice of bread for both himself and his daughter.

As the father finished preparing the snack and was about to eat his open cuisine, he folded the bread he had spread the peanut butter on in half which prompted the daughter to ask the question. "Why do you fold yours over like that?" The father responded by saying boastfully. "Because my father use to fold his over like that and I've always wanted to do everything just like my father." The daughter responded with a loving smile. "That's silly" and immediately without realizing it, folded her bread in the same manner that she had just witnessed her father do.

As you think of the possibility that your sons and daughters, without thinking, may be engaging life in the same manner as you have demonstrated before them, I have to ask you, <u>are you ok with that?</u>

August 9, 2009

John E. Harrison

Words of Inspiration

FUNCTIONAL WRECKS

One of the questions auto insurance claims representatives ask when an accident is reported is, "is the vehicle drivable?" The drivability of the vehicle does not change the fact that it has sustained obvious damage. However it does influence the decision of the driver as to whether the vehicle will be repaired immediately or delayed to a time that is more convenient and or affordable. As a result of decisions to delay repairs we have on the streets, countless vehicles that have been wrecked but are still operational.

And likewise in the church we have countless members who have sustained obvious damages from life collisions. Damages that have left them scared, scratched and dented. But because they are still able to function, the necessary reparative measures are delayed, and as a result of decisions to delay appeals to the restorative grace of GOD, the church is filled with countless members that are nothing more than <u>FUNCTIONAL WRECKS</u>.

August 16, 2009

I DON'T THINK SO

GOD has provided what I like to refer to as a forgiveness provision in first John the first chapter and the ninth verse. Here is how it works….the first step is that there must be an acknowledgement of personal or individual sin. The provision is then activated by confession of that sin resulting in forgiveness and cleaning from all unrighteousness.

However, because this forgiveness provision is so rarely used we might be tempted to believe that it is no longer needed.

WHAT DO YOU THINK?

IF YOU ASKED ME, I DON'T THINK SO

August 23, 2009

Words of Inspiration

LEADER'S FRUSTRATION

One of the things that serve as a source of frustration for committed leaders is that of uncommitted followers. This is not an issue that is unique to the corporate world it is also a serious concern within the church. Therefore the polling question before those of us in the church is "Am I a source of support or a cause of frustration for my leader?"

The process is simple. Just respond to the following questions.

Where am I on the night when my church is conducting bible study?

Where am I when my church is participating in its mid-week or missionary services?

Where was I am on Sundays that happen to fall on holidays, birthdays, anniversaries, or just need a break?

Am I doing the things I know to do or only those things I am asked to do?

When have I heard the call to worship in my church?

Words of Inspiration

When was the last time I informed my leader that I was not going to be present and available to carry out my duties during a regularly scheduled ministry activity?

If your answers to these questions place you outside of your place of duty and or direct support of and participation in the ministry functions of the church you have joined; Then it is reasonable to suggest that you are a direct contribution to your spiritual <u>LEADER'S FRUSTRATION</u>

September 6, 2009

WHAT IF

What if GOD only spoke to those who responded in obedience?

What if GOD only called those who would respond with here am I send me?

What if GOD only blessed those who practiced being a blessing to others?

What if GOD only loved those who demonstrated love toward others?

What if GOD only had time for those who demonstrated patience with others?

If GOD only responded to those who were always available to do whatever they could to meet the needs of others, what would be the level of his interaction with you?

September 13, 2009

Words of Inspiration

IT DEPENDS ON THE CIRCUMSTANCES

Many people who have been wronged by others, when asked about their attitude toward forgiveness would respond, "It depends on the circumstances" what if when we come to GOD broken and contrite, seeking his forgiveness his response to our petition was based on <u>circumstances.</u>

September 20, 2009

John E. Harrison

Words of Inspiration

GOD'S LOVE REMAINS CONSTANT

In a world where change has become the catch phrase of the season, life can more and more be defined by its constant inconsistencies; changes in relationships, changes in vocational pursuits, changes in views and values. Changes in life goals, changes in family structures, changing churches, changing partners, changing minds about changes made and the list goes on. But in the midst of an ever changing world one thing is certain;

<u>GOD'S love remains constant</u>.

September 27, 2009

Words of Inspiration

A PRAYER OF SURRENDERED WILL

My idea of a great tragedy is to be blessed with abundance only to become selfish and uncompassionate for the concerns of others.

"All that I have Lord I place at your disposal…I will do whatever you say"

October 4, 2009

Words of Inspiration

IN MOMENTS LIKE THESE

The trials of our present ought to be

for the purpose of validating

the strength of our relationship,

the test of what time has taught

us are revealed in moments like these.

October 11, 2009

Words of Inspiration

HELP ME HOLY GHOST

When I think of my imperfections in the light of the scripture that commands, "Be ye also perfect even as your father in heaven is perfect." All I can say is that I have a long way to go…

<u>HELP ME HOLY GHOST!</u>

October 18, 2009

Words of Inspiration

CONFESS YOUR SINS

There is only one thing that I can think of that is worse than sins committed and that is sins unconfessed.

"If you confess your sins GOD is faithful and just to forgive your sins and to cleanse you from all unrighteousness." I John 1:9

October 25, 2009

Words of Inspiration

LEGACY VERSUS FAULTS

Most men's true legacy will not be known

or appreciated until after they are dead,

while they are living, we are too busy

FOCUSING ON THEIR FAULTS.

November 1, 2009

Words of Inspiration

IT'S A MATTER OF CHOICE

When life has dealt you a blow that lands you in posture of defeat, the outcome of the rest of your life hinges on whether you choose to accept a momentary setback as a life sentence.

Or

To dust yourself off and get back in the game…The choice is yours.

Winning and losing is a matter of choice.

November 8, 2009

John E. Harrison

MY CONSTANT THOUGHT

As I faced the many challenges that are consistent with life's unfolding, tempted toward discouragement, overwhelmed by the demands of duty; Two thoughts, which are one of the same. Repeatedly played back in my mind like a scratched 45 record from back in the day. This thought was so constant that it would not allow me to forget that. GOD is good…All the time.

November 15, 2009

Words of Inspiration

IT'S NOT OVER UNTIL YOU QUIT

Defeat can be defined as giving up before you have gained the victory. The bible says the race is not given to the swift or the victory to the strong, but to the ones who endure to the end. Therefore you cannot be declared a looser as long as you are engaged in the battle… so,

<u>FIGHT ON, IT'S NOT OVER UNTIL YOU QUIT.</u>

November 22, 2009

Words of Inspiration

REAFFIRM YOUR LOVE DAILY

The certainty of your love and commitment to your family and or friends should never be a matter of question. You should

<u>REAFFIRM IT EVERY DAY.</u>

November 29, 2009

John E. Harrison

Words of Inspiration

AN OPPORTUNITY TO FORGIVE

Hurt for no reason , lied on, denied your rights, ripped off, robbed, violated, falsely accused, excluded, used, kicked when you are down, talked down to, written off as not worthy, not worthy of love, not worthy of respect, not worthy of support, not worthy of the kindness of others, conditional love, denied love, controlled by esteem, manipulated in misery. Each provides a perfect opportunity to forgive.

December 27, 2009

Words of Inspiration

OUR JOY, OUR BURDEN

THE PAINS , THE HURTS, THE DISAPPOINTMENTS, THE STRUGGLES, THE SETBACKS, THE BROKENNESS, THE LACK , THE LOSSES, THE FEARS, THE LET DOWNS, THE BREAKUPS, THE BREAKDOWNS , THE UPS ,THE DOWNS, THE POSITIVE AND THE NEGATIVE EXPERIENCES IN THE LIVES OF OTHERS ARE NOT TO BE BORNE BY ONE,THEY ARE TO BE SHARED BY ALL.

January 3, 2010

Words of Inspiration

My Goal, My Enemy - My Brother

My goals for 2010 include spending time in prayer daily on behalf of my enemies that our relationship would be transformed into that of Friends, or

Better Still…Brothers.

January 10, 2010

Words of Inspiration

Succeeding By Doing Nothing

The call of God on our lives is often so inconsistent with the way we see ourselves in the natural. And as a result of this inconsistency of perspectives, we allow our sense of natural abilities, or inabilities to interfere with our divine purpose.

> We allow our personal struggles to overrule or nullify our God given potential.

> We allow our present flaws to disqualify us as contestants for future pursuits.

> And consequently, we alter our course, choosing shortcuts that lead to nowhere,

> REQUIRNG NOTHING AS A CRITERIA FOR SUCCESS.

January 17, 2010

John E. Harrison

Words of Inspiration

I Should Have Prayed For the City

As I Traveled down Buena Vista Road on New Year's Eve, misty rain, reckless drivers moving hastily on their way, congested traffic, foggy, limited visibility, I feared for my safety and the safety of the motorist whose destination directed them that way and therefore, I prayed that God would cover and protect the motorist who traveled this potentially dangerous street.

As I traveled down St. Mary's Road on my way home, I immediately observed a police car with blue lights flashing, two cars pulled over, baby seat being transferred from one car to another...an accident!

A sick feeling came over me that identified just how limited and selfish I had been in my previous prayer. The first thought that came to my mind was,

"I SHOULD HAVE PRAYED FOR THE CITY, NOT JUST A STREET WITHIN IT."

January 24, 2010

John E. Harrison

Words of Inspiration

ISSUES OF THE HEART

THE FAILURE OF ONE'S PARTNER TO MEASURE UP TO CERTAIN EXPECTATION OR TO FULFILL CERTAIN DESIRE IS ALWAYS AN ISSUE THAT DISRUPTS HARMONY WITHIN THE MARRIAGE RELATIONSHIP.

IF ANY MARRIAGE IS GOING TO WORK AND DEVELOP INTO A PEACEFUL AND HEALTHY ALLIANCE, THERE MUST COME A TIME WHEN COUPLES MUST SETTLE IN THEIR OWN MINDS THAT THEIR RELATIONSHIP IS WHAT IT IS AND RESOLVE TO ACCEPT ONE ANOTHER FOR WHO THEY ARE, THE WAY THEY ARE.

FROM THAT POINT ON THE PERCEIVED FLAWS OF ONE'S PARTNER ARE NO LONGER TO BE SUBJECTS DEALT WITH VIA DISCUSSION, INSTEAD THEY ARE MATTERS TO BE DEALT WITH AS ISSUES OF THE HEART.

January 31, 2010

John E. Harrison

Words of Inspiration

Compassion Fatigue

The story an Army psychiatrist who pulled out a loaded weapon, shot and killed more than a dozen of his comrades while processing to depart the United States to serve a tour in the Middle East was attributed to what is known of as compassion fatigue.

Compassion fatigue in laymen's terms is nothing more than becoming tired of demonstrating concern for those who are hurting either physically, spiritually, emotionally or financially. It is the outgrowth of well-doing that has become weary.

Could it be that the obvious lack of concern for the pains that continues to be the bedfellows of so many who sit beside us in churches on Sunday morning is a creeping in of the outgrowth of that same well-doing that has become weary?

Could it be that the church, with all of its hoopla and fanfare.

With all of its bold leaping without brotherly love.

With all of its cheap talk without costly involvement.

John E. Harrison

Words of Inspiration

Is actually a demonstration of symptoms that are akin to that Texas shooter who had become weary of his involvement in the struggles of others; and in like manner, in desperate need of a divine intervention.

May the Spirit of the loving Christ fill our hearts with His love.

February 7, 2010

Words of Inspiration

Nothing to Speak About

As I went about the normal routine of my day I did a lot of thinking about needs, struggles, and concerns of others.

I thought about a sister recovering from surgery.

I thought about people suffering in Haiti.

I thought about mothers struggling to provide for their children.

I thought about young men searching for employment but finding nothing.

I thought about the incarcerated.

The home bound

The lonely

The mentally ill

The unloved

The bereaved

The homeless

John E. Harrison

Words of Inspiration

At the end of the day I thought about what I had done to provide support, demonstrate concern or provide help in some small way for those whose concerns I had pondered and there was nothing there to speak about.

And then I thought "I will let my thoughts of today establish my agenda for tomorrow."

February 21, 2010

Words of Inspiration

OTHER THAN THAT, IT WAS FINE

At the end of the day as we arrive at home we are often met with a greeting followed by the question, "How was your day?" A honest response would look like this.....

I shirked responsibility;

I misrepresented truth;

I laughed at filthy jokes;

I failed to speak out against unfair treatment;

I denied a co-worker help, when I saw she clearly needed it;

I made negative statements about a fellow employee;

I talked about my boss;

I checked my personal e-mail fifteen times;

I sent ten text messages;

I took two extra minutes on each of my breaks;

I returned from lunch five minutes late.

<u>Other than that, it was fine.</u>

February 28, 2010

John E. Harrison

Words of Inspiration

He Always Gives Another Chance

For those who are prone and known for your mess-ups, you have probably heard the phrase...

I am going to help you out this time, but this is your last chance, with man chances are limited but with God it's different.

HE ALWAYS GIVES YOU ANOTHER CHANCE.

March 7, 2010

Words of Inspiration

He Will Supply

Today I am faced with the same needs for daily sustenance as in days passed but my faith is shaken due to faults in my faithfulness. But then I remembered that even when I fail to live up to God's expectations of me He will always provide those things I need of Him.

IN SPITE OF MY FAILINGS, HE WILL SUPPLY

March 14, 2010

Thank You

For my health as well as it is; my home, my family, my children, my grandchildren, my husband, my wife, my friends, my means of income for bills paid, food, clothing, a source of transporting, a friend who shares a ride for prayer partners, for books to read, for an inspirational word when I am feeling down, for committed relationships, for sins forgiven, for salvation assured, for sickness and not death, for the strength that follows weakness, for joy after sadness, for reconciliation after disputes, for restoration after brokenness, for healing assured after sickness endured, for rest after labor, for a savior who loves me, who lived to die for me, who paid for my sins in full, and for time spent in your presence, Lord…

THANK YOU.

March 21, 2010

Words of Inspiration

Count Your Blessings

It has been said that counting sheep will help you overcome episodes of insomnia, however if you have never developed a fondness for sheep another option would be to count other things, your money, your bills, your enemies, the times you have failed to succeed in your endeavors, the number of times you have had to apologize for the same misdeed, or you could do as I do and

COUNT YOUR BLESSINGS.

March 28, 2010

NO SUBSTITUTE

I heard an interesting statement a few days ago that captured my attention and caused me to seriously ponder the implications of what I had heard.

There is a substitute for everything; for sugar we have Sweet and Low, the pink pack, Sweeter, Equal, and Splendor. For butter there is; I Can't Believe it's Not Butter, Margarine, and Whipped Spreads. For Milk there is Silk. For Real Motor Oils there are synthetics. For real worship we have praise and worship song services. For love we have sex. For commitment in relationships, even to Christ, we have participation in external activities such as living together instead of marriage. Attending church instead of falling in love with Jesus.

These substitutes are able to satisfy the taste buds, to lubricate the machine, to appease the spiritual and yes the physical appetite. But when I looked for a substitute that could settle the redemptive debt for the sins of fallen man, I found none; only Christ on the cross could do that, and for the Christ of the Cross… **THERE IS NO SUBSTITUTE!**

April 4, 2010

John E. Harrison

Words of Inspiration

IS THE PROBLEM

WORTH THE CONFLICT?

Many other things that disrupt and ultimately destroy relationships are problems that have been addressed but unsuccessfully resolved.

Many of these unresolved disputes between once friends, married couples, family members, co-workers and yes, fellow Christians which have lead to broken fellowship could have been easily avoided if, before attempting to confront another based upon dissenting opinion, consideration had been,

"Is The Problem Worth The Conflict?"

April 11, 2010

Words of Inspiration

His Reflection

When I reflect upon God

and his character I see my goal.

So that when he reflects upon me,

he will see

His Reflection.

April 27, 2010

John E. Harrison

Words of Inspiration

Dark Spots in the Heart

There is no question about my salvation; I am certain of my conversion experience. However there is this matter of darkness in my heart...

Deception, dishonesty, unfaithfulness, pride, unforgiveness, anger, envying, greed, lust unthankfulness, lack of consideration of others, legalistic, mean spirited and oft...times uncaring.

Yes...my soul is saved, but as for this matter of darkness I pray, "Lord let the dark dispelling light of you Word fill my heart that it may be as pure as my salvation is certain

May 2, 2010

Words of Inspiration

HE HEARS YOU

When the storm of life is raging so loud that you cannot hear yourself think, God can still hear the whisper of your prayer.

Fear not. You are not alone.

<u>He hears you</u>.

May 9, 2010

Words of Inspiration

God Always Keeps His Word

When you think that no one is aware of your struggles, God is.

When you think that no one can feel the hurt in your heart, God can.

When you think that there is no way out of the situation you are in, God is the way.

When you think that no one can hear the silence of your tears, God hears.

When you think that you are alone in your valley of what seems like death,

God is right there with you.

You are not alone.

Remember, He promised never to leave you nor forsake you,

    AND HE ALWAYS KEEPS HIS WORD

        May 15, 2010

Words of Inspiration

Play Like It … And Do It

If I ruled the world I would seek to know the heart of its Creator.

To understand and support His vision for its inhabitants.

To apply His wisdom to the resolution of every conflict. I would allow myself to be touched by every infirmity.

To experience every sorrow. To feel every pain. I would love the unlovable. Forgive the unspeakable. Champion the underdog. Embrace the repulsive. Believe in the careless. With the mindless... Share wisdom

However

My reality is, I don't rule the world, but my choice is to…

PLAY LIKE I DO AND

<u>DO THESE THINGS ANY-HOW.</u>

May 23, 2010

John E. Harrison

Words of Inspiration

EXPRESS YOURSELF

Living in the presence of those who you would consider to be your enemies provides a greater opportunity for you to be a living expression of the commonly used phrase,

"God Loves you and so do I."

So go ahead...EXPRESS YOURSELF

May 30, 2010

Words of Inspiration

I Play Chicken and Hide

When I am compassed about by the calamities of life; encircled by the wickedness of the host of my enemies...

I PLAY CHICKEN...AND HIDE UNDER THE SHADOW OF GOD'S WINGS.

Psalm 17:8

June 6, 2010

John E. Harrison

Words of Inspiration

Whatcha Looking At?

It is interesting how God can look at man and see potential and possibility. While man can look at man and see one who is not worthy of worth. How can it be that God can see the best in you when everyone else around you can only see the worst in you? It is because God alone reserves the right to look within you.

While everyone else around you are simply looking at you. And the truth is they don't have a clue as to what they are looking at.

June 13, 2010

Words of Inspiration

That Was So Love

The adverb so describes something that is more than average in its ability to capture attention and stimulate memory for an extended period of time.

That meal was so good

The sunset was so beautiful

The words to the song were so touching

The sales representative was so helpful

The trip to the amusement park was so fun

God giving His Son to die for my sins...

NOW THAT WAS SOOOO LOVE!

John 3:16

June 20, 2010

He Gave More

I sought God for healing, He gave me wholeness.

I sought His protection, He became my fortress.

I sought His face, He revealed Himself.

I sought Him for a new beginning, He gave me new life.

In all of the things that I have sought God for

"HE HAS ALWAYS GIVEN MORE THAN I'VE ASKED."

Ephesians 3:20

June 27, 2010

I'll Get Back With You

When faced with a problem that demanded wisdom that took me

Beyond the scope of my experience; my immediate response was

To pray and seek Gods' guidance in the matter.

My prayer was simple….It went like this, "Lord what shall I Do?"

His response was immediate and unmistakably clear.

It went like this, "Wait right there, and don't do NOTHING until you hear from me.

<u>I'll get back with you.</u>"

July 4, 2010

John E. Harrison

Words of Inspiration

When Stuff Happens

As a couple traveled on their way to participate in a family reunion, enjoying the quiet peace of their spirits as they distanced themselves from the demands of everyday duty and responsibility, their thoughts were filled with the anticipation of seeing relatives whose company they had not experienced and enjoyed for too long.

Their lives were centered on themselves. They were consumed by the thought of anticipated and well deserved pleasure, when, in the near distance a lone SUV swerved and for no obvious reason, began to flip over and over and over, slinging and banging its occupants like a rag doll against the lightly padded interior, finally coming to rest after five violet revolutions.

With that scene before them, their lives were no longer centered on themselves. They were no longer consumed by thoughts of personal pleasure.

Instead they were swallowed up by the need represented by the scene before them. And with all of the energy that had once been focused on themselves, they began to pull mangled bodies from that wreckage praying with all earnest that the God

of their faith would honor their presence and preserve the lives of those unnamed passengers.

When stuff happens to other folk, will you be willing to shift your focus from yourself and your personal pursuit of pleasure and allow yourself to be consumed by the need before you?

July 11, 2010

Words of Inspiration

WHERE DID THAT COME FROM

After having endured a tense conversation with someone whose opinion of me is way less than favorable, being careful not to say anything that would destroy my credibility as a Christian, without thinking, my closing statement was, "I Love You, Be Blessed."

Witnessing the words that came from my mouth, my immediate response was, "Where did that come from?"

John 12:34 reveals that "Out of the Abundance of the Heart, The Mouth Speaketh." So I guess it must have come from my heart.

July 18, 2010

Words of Inspiration

YOUR HARVEST IS IN YOUR SEED

Scripture is clear that there is an undeniable association between sowing and reaping.

The implication is that outcome has to do with input.

Therefore, you cannot live a destructive life and expect to have mountain top experiences.

What you nurture is what you will produce.

The moral to this story is…

<u>THE HARVEST YOU REAP IS BASED SOLELY ON THE SEED YOU SOW</u>

July 25, 2010

John E. Harrison

Words of Inspiration

IT'S GOOD TO KNOW JESUS

When your car breaks down, it's good to know a capable mechanic.

When your toilets are backing up, it's good to know a plumber.

When you are faced with serious health issues, it's good to know a medical specialist.

When you consider the question of the Eternal Redemption of your fallen soul,

IT'S GOOD TO KNOW JESUS!

                      August 1, 2010

Words of Inspiration

YOU CAN HANDLE IT

Feeling burdened, overwhelmed, like you are dealing with more than you can handle?

Don't be deceived by sensory perceptions. Take heart, and remember God will not allow you to be tempted beyond that which you are able to bear; but will, with every temptation provide a way of escape that you may be able to bear it.

In this case your escape is in the way you think. Not in the way you feel. Therefore, think on the promises and stand in the authority of His word. His word says, "YOU CAN HANDLE IT."

August 8, 2010

John E. Harrison

THE WORD IS YOUR VICTORY

If you are to exercise absolute authority over the works of the devil, God's word must have absolute authority over your life; your thoughts, your words, your deeds. The only way to guarantee a win every time is to play by the rules all the time.

While it is not possible to avoid the offensive attacks of the devil it is possible to avoid becoming a victim of his successes.

<u>The Word Is Your Victory</u>.

August 15, 2010

Words of Inspiration

PROMISE KEEPERS, COVENANT BREAKERS

Two kinds of people: Promise Keepers, Covenant Breakers… Two kinds of people are mentioned often in scripture, those who make promises and keep them and those who make promises and break them.

A covenant is initiated with a word of promise and is established when that word is tested.

If your word is kept during the testing then the covenant you have initiated is established.

Two kinds of people

PROMISE KEEPERS, COVENANT BREAKERS

Of the two, which kind are you?

August 22, 2010

John E. Harrison

ONE THING THOU LACKETH

It is impossible to be totally sold out for God, living a life of total surrender, yet still court separate agendas in what we refer to as our personal lives. If your personal life is not also surrendered to Him, then none of your life is accepted by Him.

<u>It's really about all or nothing!</u>

August 29, 2010

Words of Inspiration

That Sounds So like Christ

If you have ever been wounded as a result of the sins of others and the pain just won't go away

Try Forgiveness.

Forgiveness will take away your pain and heal the hurt so effectively until all that is left are the scares.

<u>That sounds soooo like Christ, into whose image and likeness you are being conformed.</u>

September 5, 2010

Words of Inspiration

Darkness Is As Light To Him

If you ever find yourself in a place of darkness and you cannot see your way out, just know that your situation is not a challenge for God. Just ask Him to hold your hand and He will get you through it.

You see

DARKNESS IS AS LIGHT TO HIM.

September 12, 2010

Words of Inspiration

Accept No Gifts from the Devil

The bible tells us that every good and perfect gift comes from God. Therefore, when I am tempted to become intimidated, and fearful as I am confronted with the many challenges of life, I remind myself that "God did not give me the spirit of fear, but of power and of love and a sound mind."

If fear is not of God it must be of the devil and I refuse to accept his gift.

September 19, 2010

Words of Inspiration

JOY AT DAY BREAK

Great wisdom can be the birth-child of great failure. Great faith can be the outgrowth of great suffering. Great joy can be the after effects of great sorrow.

One writer put it this way;

"It is good for me that I have been afflicted; that I might learn thy statues."

Again at the dedication of the House of David, this declaration of hope was made;

"Weeping may endure for a night, but joy cometh in the morning." Therefore, don't be surprised when you have wiped away the tears of your night of weeping and are able to get a clear view of the day ahead that you discover joy, <u>Unspeakable Joy Being Released with the Breaking of Day.</u>

September 26, 2010

Words of Inspiration

IN MOMENTS LIKE THESE

The trials of our present ought to be for the purpose of validating the strength of our relationships, the test of what time has taught us is revealed in moments like these.

October 4, 2010

Words of Inspiration

BRIDGES OR WALLS

Two kinds of builders come to mind when I think of the common approach to resolving conflict. Those who build walls and those who build bridges. Wall builders tend to be closed minded unwilling to consider things from the perspective of another thus forcing two people to remain on descending sides of an issue.

Bridge builder, on the other hand tends to create an atmosphere that welcomes a mutual exchange that allows for a sharing of opinions; gleaning from the social interactions of two persons who share opposing opinion, substance that can be used to arrive at a place of reconciliation.

With that having been said, The question is?...Are you A Builder of Walls that Perpetuates Separation or A Builder of Bridges that Leads to Reconciliation?

October 17, 2010

I AM TRYING

I try to treat everyone with fairness and equality. I try to love everybody without regard for reciprocation.

I try to respond with empathy to things that I neither fully understand nor totally agree

I try to balance my life in a manner that insures that no area of my life is neglected or ignored to the point of deterioration.

I try to insure, by word and deed, that the people who God has placed in my life are aware of my appreciation of them all.

I try not to waste one precious moment of the time that God has allowed me to remain here on earth focusing on negativity. Groveling in triviality or pondering pessimism.

I try to give God my best in His service every day.

I try to love and provide for my family without attempts to control or limit their freedom to be...

I try to model lifestyle and behavior in a manner that will influence both the young and the not so young to always strive for more Christ likeness in their own experience.

John E. Harrison

Words of Inspiration

I try to be a voice of wisdom to those who seek my counsel.

I try to respond to false accusations and unfair treatment with love and forgiveness.

I try to stand in integrity in spite of the grandiose promises of present temptation.

I TRY

I cannot say that I have succeeded in any of the efforts that I have listed, but I can say with clearness of conscience that **I AM TRYING.**

October 24, 2010

THINK

The one major contributor to the disruption of harmony between those who are engaged in building healthy relationships is…making hasty comments that have not been censored by the wisdom of the word nor approved by the spirit of God. So if you find yourself with blanket and pillow in hand spending frequent nights in the front room, or living what should be your happiest days engaged in a cold war in that place that should represent a bit of heaven on earth as a result of your thoughtless verbiage and you really would like for the cycle to end. The answer is so simple a caveman can do it.

THINK BEFORE YOU SPEAK!

November 2, 2010

Words of Inspiration

SOMETIMES

Sometime I don't feel like forgiving the wrongs that are continually directed against me.

Sometimes I feel like the call upon my life is a sentence that dooms me to isolation and loneliness without opportunity for genuine social interaction with peers who can be depended upon to provide support and encouragement in the everyday struggles of life.

Sometimes I feel more like I am being tolerated rather than appreciated.

Sometimes I feel a great sense of abandonment by those who once pledged support of the vision that God has called us to.

Sometime I don't feel like going home to confusion, attitudes, accusations, negativity, vacillating commitments.

Sometimes I wonder how expressions of love can be limited to special days that are sprinkled throughout the year and ignored during the times that exist in between.

Sometimes I feel like the commitment to the work of ministry is distributed with inequity with the expectation that the majority of the work and over watch be the responsibility of the minority.

John E. Harrison

Words of Inspiration

Sometimes I feel like a stranger existing on the outskirts of a city that should be viewed as my home…with declining connections with a family that spans and populates my Father's Kingdom.

Sometimes I feel that pungent piercing pain of subtle disrespect and total disregard for authority with such intensity that it robs me of rest presses my heart to breaking while saturating it with tears.

Sometimes I wonder with amazement at how Jesus endured so much and still remained undeniably positive and persistent in His pursuit of purpose.

And I resolve to be more like Him,

<u>Not Sometimes but All the Time…</u>

November 7, 2010

Words of Inspiration

BECAUSE I SAID I DO

When things are not going the way I know it should in my home and I feel like lashing out, releasing my frustration in the form of unrestrained verbal expressions

I DON'T.

When I measure the minimal progress that my maximum efforts are producing as I give my life in labor for the betterment of the family that God has given and I feel like going for a long drive to an undisclosed destination with an undermined date of return seeking escape from the reality of it all

I DON'T.

When I feel like retreating into a place of total silence refraining from all communications because so little of my thoughts and concerns are heard and understood

I DON'T.

When the golden rule becomes an obvious tool that is being used for personal gain and I am tempted to adopt "AN EYE FOR AN EYE, A TOOTH FOR A TOOTH" as my motto...

Words of Inspiration

I DON'T.

I DON'T BECAUSE, WHEN ASKED, AS I STOOD BEFORE GOD AND MAN, DO YOU PROMISE TO HAVE THIS WOMAN TO BE THY WEDDED WIFE, TO LIVE TOGETHER AFTER GOD'S ORDINANCE IN THE HOLY ESTATE OF MATRIMONY? DO YOU PROMISE TO LOVE HER, COMFORT HER, HONOR AND KEEP HER, IN SICKNESS AND IN HEALTH: FORSAKING ALL OTHERS, KEEPING THEE ONLY UNTO HER, SO LONG AS YE BOTH SHALL LIVE?

I SAID "I DO."

November 14, 2010

John E. Harrison

Words of Inspiration

That Bothers Me

When my only means of transportation was failing and I was forced to park in a manner insuring that I would be able to drive forward because my transmission reverse did not work.

That didn't bother me.

When the unfolding of life events affected my financial status in such a way that I could not pay my bills.

That didn't bother me.

When I was diagnosed with diabetes with a mandate to re-structure my pattern of living so as to continue to fulfill the call that God has on my life with the same level of diligence.

That didn't bother me.

When faith to believe that God could sustain us in a time of declining support was challenged and shaken.

That didn't bother me.

Words of Inspiration

BUT WHEN I LOOK AT THE SUBTLE DETERIORATION OF THE LOVE AND COMMITMENT THAT SHOULD HOLD A BROTHERHOOD TOGETHER.

<u>THAT BOTHERS ME</u>

November 21, 2010

Words of Inspiration

SOW AND WAIT

THE LAW OF SEED TIME AND HARVEST IS TWOFOLD.

THE FIRST STEP IS TO SOW AND KEEP ON SOWING.

THE SECOND STEP IS TO WAIT AND KEEP ON WAITING.

YOUR HARVEST IS THE FRUIT OF YOUR ENDURANCE.

November 28, 2010

Words of Inspiration

THE POWER OF LISTENING

As I sat at my work space dominated by the demands of modern technology, I was joined in that space by a young man expressing feelings of hurts, disappointments of the past, feelings of having been rejected by family, denied the opportunity to establish lasting relationships with others because of the instability that has always been consistent with his existence.

As he disclosed details of deep personal hurts and disappointments that has left him timid, angry, untrusting of others and fearful to believe in his own ability to experience life on a greater level of quality, I quietly pushed myself back and away from my desk and faced him as he spoke, making frequent eye contact, nodding with gestures to insure that my attending to what was being said was obvious and without question.

After about five minutes of self disclosing, with a broad expression he sighed of relief written on his face and said;

"I'M NOT GOING TO TAKE UP ANY MORE OF YOUR TIME.

I FEEL BETTER NOW.

John E. Harrison

Words of Inspiration

<u>Thank you for listening.</u>"

Could it be that we frequently mishandle opportunities to help others feel better simply because we have not discovered

<u>THE POWER OF LISTENING?</u>

December 19, 2010

Words of Inspiration

CAN I TRUST YOU?

THE RAW, UNCUT REALITIES OF OUR INDIVIDUAL STRUGGLES SHOULD NOT BE BURDENS THAT WE ARE FORCED TO BEAR ALONE SIMPLY BECAUSE OF THE UNRESOLVED QUESTION;

<u>CAN I TRUST YOU WITH THE TRUTH OF MY REALITY?</u>

December 26, 2010

Words of Inspiration

THE NORMAL CHRISTIAN LIFE

"I CAN'T" IS A RELEVANT STATEMENT AS LONG AS I LIVE IN A NATURAL REALITY, BUT WHEN I COME TO THE PLACE OF NOT "I" BUT CHRIST LIVES IN ME…. THEN ALL OF MY, I CAN NOTS BECOME I CAN DO ALL THING THROUGH CHRIST WHO STRENGTHENS ME.

January 2, 2011

Words of Inspiration

MY MORTALITY, HIS PURPOSE

IF MY DEATH SATISFIES GOD'S PURPOSE,

THEN I LIVE WITH MY LIFE CONSTANTLY BEING OFFERED UP,

WAITING TO HEAR HIS CALL.

January 9, 2011

HIS WONDERS

I asked God for rest, He increased my labor.

I asked God for comfort in my home, He allowed unrest.

I asked God for peace, He allowed trouble to overtake me.

I asked God for friends, He allowed my enemy to encamp all around me.

I asked God, how long? He said, until I have completed the work I started in you.

The Lord works in mysterious ways;

<u>His wonders to perform</u>.

                              January 16, 2011

Words of Inspiration

When I Am Weak

When I am feeling helpless, overwhelmed by the natural unfolding of life I pray, Lord helps me.

When my wisdom is not sufficient for the challenges before me and I cannot see my way I pray, Lord lead me.

When I am feeling frail, mentally wearied, spiritually drained and the weaknesses of this body of clay are being visibly manifested to the disgrace of my redeeming Lord I pray,

Lord let your strength be made perfect in me.

January 23, 2011

John E. Harrison

Words of Inspiration

Thinking versus Doing

I thought about the struggles that so many people are confronted with and how blessed I am to be among those who are more fortunate.

Then I remembered the sale at the mall, rushed out and purchased an outfit to compliment the shoes and purse I bought some time ago.

I thought about the struggles that so many from among us are dealing with as they battle sustained illnesses and how blessed I am that I and my family are all healthy and enjoying promised abundance.

Then I remembered that it had been weeks since I had got away just to enjoy some time of leisure, so I gas up my car, inventoried my plastic friends and set out on a leisure drive with an agenda that included a meal at a nice restaurant, shopping for nothing in Particular, returning home feeling fulfilled and refreshed.

I thought about my pattern of thinking, how my thoughts are always focused on the needs and struggles of others.

John E. Harrison

Then I remembered that while my thinking has been about others, my deeds have all been centered on me.

January 30, 2011

Words of Inspiration

I Developed Into My Thoughts

When I witnessed the fall of a fellow Christian, I immediately thought; how could he allow himself to do such a thing? As I listened with uninterrupted attention as the ministry vision was being presented, I immediately thought; we will never accomplish that. As I sat quietly listening to my thoughts, I realized that I have become judgmental, and critical; without compassion for the struggles of others, my faith and faithfulness has given way to a dim pessimistic view of life, even with God as its source of supply and direction. Then it dawned on me that, <u>I have developed into my thoughts</u>.

February 6, 2011

John E. Harrison

Words of Inspiration

Your Uniqueness Challenged My Weakness

I have always interacted comfortably and confidently with those who I share things in common, but because you are different I find myself being tempted and pulled in both positive and negative directions. To love you, to lust after you, to accept you, to reject you, to explore out of curiosity, to trust you, to doubt your trustworthiness, to welcome you here, to wish you were there, to include, to exclude, to find commonalities, to confirm incompatibilities.

All that is weak and prematurely developed within me is challenged when I am confronted by someone who is not like me or those who form my circle of associates.

February 13, 2011

John E. Harrison

Words of Inspiration

Praise Keeps You Focused

Should there be a connection between what you are experiencing internally and what you are giving off externally?

Should your burdens affect your behavior?

Should the weight on your shoulders effect the expressions on your face?

Should the things with which you are confronted change your countenance, or Should your external expressions remain constant in spite of your internal struggles?

In Psalms 34:1, David revealed his strategy for insuring that life's changes did not change his attitude toward life by blessing and praising God in the midst of his most challenging experiences.

Herein is his secret revealed

"I will bless the Lord at all times; his praises shall continually be in my mouth."

February 20, 2011

Words of Inspiration

Making Things Happen

Many of the goals that we were destined to achieve in life are never reached because of a failure to coordinate a rendezvous with ideal circumstances and perfect opportunities.

Red Foxx of Sanford and Son had a word of wisdoms for those whose purpose may be held up as you wait for things to come together as a result of the natural unfolding of life.

Foxx said, "Sometimes opportunity knocks, while at other times you have to call him up and invite him over to your house."

In other words, there are times when you can wait for things to happen while at other times you become responsible for <u>making things happen.</u>

February 27, 2011

John E. Harrison

Words of Inspiration

Discipline versus Destruction

One of the most difficult challenges for parents is to discipline their child.

One of the most destructive things parents can do is fail to do so.

Proverbs 19:18

Chasten your son while there is hope, and do not set your heart on his destruction.

Proverbs 22:6

Train ups a child in the way he should go, and when he is old he will not depart from it.

March 6, 2011

Words of Inspiration

Now That I Think About It, We Are Not That Different

As I move purposefully between vocation and ministry duties, it is often the case that I find myself being held up by some old person driving thirty five miles per hour in the lane that has been designated the "slow lane."

My response to such interruptions to my purpose driven life is to wish that they had a law restricting the times that old people were authorized to drive to the non rush hour parts of the day.

Then I remembered if that were the case I wouldn't be out here.

Sometime we are more like the people we criticize than we like to admit.

March 13, 2011

Words of Inspiration

I Wanted To Do Better So I Did

There were times in my life when my manner of living fell consistently outside of the scope of my understanding of the will of God for my life, and

I wanted to do better, so I did.

In other words, if you want to do better at living a better life, God will help you, but you have to do it.

March 20, 2011

Words of Inspiration

I Would Give Anything

There are sinful enticements that you may be willing to give anything for the privilege of indulging in its decadent allure. Anything in this context, relates to a select part or portion of one's total possessions.

However, sin is never satisfied with the <u>ANYTHING THAT YOU ARE WILLING TO GIVE,</u> its goal is to destroy everything that you possess

March 27, 2011

Words of Inspiration

Don't Do It

Satan can only suggest or insinuate he can only sow a seed of doubt in your mind. It is up to you what you allow to proceed from your mind to your heart.

Satan can coerce but he cannot command or control your actions. He can persuade through intellectual reasoning, but you have to decide to participate in his schemes.

My suggestion to you is: DON'T DO IT.

April 3, 2011

Words of Inspiration

My Tears Are For Me

My tears are shed for me, not for you.

For my release not for your response.

While you may view my tears as evidence of your power to hurt me,

the greater truth is,

they are a demonstration of God's power to comfort and release me.

Therefore

MY TEARS ARE SHED FOR ME,

NOT FOR YOU.

April 10, 2011

John E. Harrison

Words of Inspiration

Talk To Me...I Won't Tell

Feeling overwhelmed, like I am being pulled apart by the demands of life. Thoughts of my reality rushing, racing through my mind. Thoughts that I dare not share with even my closet friend.

What a feeling, so much going on inside and no one to talk to about it.

Then God said "YOU CAN TALK TO ME, THAT WAY NO ONE'S CONFIDENCE WILL BE BETRAYED."

April 24, 2011

Your Second Thought

If God has inspired a thought in you to do good, to bless, to partner with someone in their struggle, to sow into someone's future, don't think about it just do it. but if you just happen to be one of those people who are compelled to think about things please, after you have finished with your thinking, make sure that;

YOUR SECOND THOUGHT IS THE SAME AS YOUR FIRST.

May 1, 2011

Words of Inspiration

If I Had It to Do All Over Again, I Would Be Grateful

My life's experiences has exposed me to haters who I have had to love

Back stabbers whose backs I have had to cover

Betrayals that I have had to forgive

Needless loses that I have had to recover

Neglects that I have had to accept

Dishonor that I have had to endure.

But as I think about it

<u>IF I HAD IT TO DO ALL OVER AGAIN,</u>

I would love without restraint

I would befriend my enemy with greater diligence

I would forgive as freely as I have been forgiven

I would consider my loses as gain

I would seek only to serve, not to be served

John E. Harrison

Words of Inspiration

I would consider dishonor an honor that identifies me with Christ.

AND BE GRATEFUL

May 8, 2011

Words of Inspiration

ASSAULT ON TRUTH

One of the most unwelcomed dialogues between man and man is godly counsel during a time of anger.

During those times truth stands but it doesn't stabilize.

It represents and points to right but it is rejected.

It hurts; therefore it, and the bearer of it, is often met with **BRUTAL ASSAULT**.

In times like these would Jesus do?

May 15, 2011

Words of Inspiration

I Tried Harder

I wanted to make a greater impact upon the plight of fallen man in his effort to remain fallen through his resolve to ignore the message of redemption through effective ministry efforts.

I wanted to build a great church, which glorified God in all things, edified man in his pursuit of purpose, and equipped leaders for effective ministry on the other side of Jordan.

I wanted to leave the world better than it was when I arrived.

I wanted my vision for a better mankind, more blessed and favored, more beneficial to the kingdom agenda to continue to be revealed long after my departure.

I wanted my works to continue to benefit man in his pursuit of God in earth as I enjoy the promise of life eternal in his presence in heaven.

It has been for these reasons that **I HAVE TRIED HARDER.**

May 22, 2011

God Hates That

There may be times when you will need someone to confide in, to vent to, to pour out your frustration in the present of. However, during those times, it becomes your responsibility to insure that the person you choose to meet that need can be trusted not to turn your words spoken in confidence into a platform for gossiping, the breeding of dissension and the spreading of discord.

Beware; God hates that.

May 29, 2011

Words of Inspiration

Wait Three Days

Sometimes things happen in our lives that cause great hurt, even anger, during those times our first inclination is to run immediately and expose our often biased version of the experience to someone close.

However, I would suggest that you hold your peace, pray over the matter for three days and after you have done that, if you are still angry it just could be that what you have experienced was God exposing your need to be more forgiving. It could just be God exposing your issues of anger, bitterness and possibly hate.

Jesus completed the process of paying the total sin debt for the whole world with every evil of man completely forgiven in three days. As his younger brothers and sisters, we should be able to forgive at least one wrong done to us within the same amount of time.

WAIT THREE DAYS

John E. Harrison

Words of Inspiration

If, after you have done that, your former issue remains a present issue it just could be that the real issue is you.

June 5, 2011

Words of Inspiration

Remove the Pebble

As I dressed myself in preparation for work, admiring the items I had chosen that accentuated the few remaining qualities of my youth. I openly thanked God for His consistent care for me.

The items I chose included a pull over, three buttons shirt with white, grey, baby blue, thin black, yellow strips; topped off with a yellow baseball cap to give a sunshine effect to my countenance. The shoes were white, starbury low cut with loose fitting jeans, a Wal-Mart fine. Overall the outfit was perfect.

However, when I stood and started to walk toward the door I felt something in my shoe that made walking uncomfortable, unnatural and unlike me.

Responding to this newly discovered discomfort I immediately sat down and removed my shoe in an attempt to find and eliminate its source. However, after two attempts the problem still remained. Determined to find and eliminate the thing that disrupted my natural stride, I persisted, and during my third attempt I also removed my sock. Turning

John E. Harrison

my thin white bamboo sock inside out I discovered a tiny pebble caught within the grip of its fabric.

As I removed the pebble from my ankle high sock, I was amazed at how such a small thing demanded such an adjustment in my walk.

If there are little things in your life that are interfering with the integrity of you stride.

Don't adjust your walk.

REMOVE THE PEBBLE

June 12, 2011

Words of Inspiration

Weakness Shrouded By Arrogance

Many people who display an abundance of strength are often the first to crumble under the pressures of life. What appears to be strength often proves to be weakness that is shrouded by an attitude of arrogance, resulting in its perpetuation as it cocoons behind an external display of toughness.

But there is hope, so don't cry about it, pray about it, and know that you can turn your weakness into strength if you will expose it to God and pray honestly about your need for His strength to be made perfect in you.

June 19, 2011

Words of Inspiration

Profile of a Godly Husband

A godly husband will remind, but will not ridicule.

Will withdraw himself, but will not withhold his love.

Will prompt to process differences for the purpose of reestablishing peace.

He is willing to pay with personal sacrifice for the negative consequences of his wife's unwise choices.

His words edify.

His love is consistent.

His communications reconciles.

He gives sacrificially

June 26, 2011

Words of Inspiration

I Can't Let'em See Me Like This

A lone elderly man stumbled, almost falling backward against a wall that could have resulted in a serious injury, unconsciousness, or even death; as he stepped out of his shower following a long yet productive day.

Because the, now dripping, untowel elderly gent had not dried his body and dawned his robe, he moved frantically to cover himself, thinking, "If something should happen to me I can't Let'em see me like this."

It was good that this vintage specimen of human creation was able to make himself more presentable as he prepared for the worst, but what about you?

What if you didn't have the opportunity to fix yourself up before meeting Christ at his judgment seat? Would you be ashamed of what He will see in you? IF so, take the time, to make preparation for that inevitable appointment by allowing the blood of Christ to cover you. That way, "He won't have to see you like that"

July 3, 2011

John E. Harrison

Words of Inspiration

A Love That Cares

It is amazing how we can claim to love so strongly and affirm that love so frequently, yet care so little. What I really need to experience in the midst of my life struggles is

A LOVE THAT CARES.

July 10, 2011

John E. Harrison

Words of Inspiration

THE CONSISTENCY OF DESIRE...THE PROBABILITY OF SIN.

HUMAN DESIRE IS CONSISTENT.

HUMAN FRAILTY IS WITHOUT PREJUDICE.

THEREFORE, THE PURSUIT OF THE FULFILLMENT OF THOSE DESIRES ARE AS CRUDE,

AS BASE AMONG THE LEARNED AS IT IS AMONG THE UNLEARNED.

AMONG THE RICH AS IT IS AMONG THE POOR.

AMONG THE POWERFUL AND AFFLUENT AS WELL AS THE WEAK AND THE INSIGNIFICANT.

AMONG LEADERS AS WELL AS FOLLOWERS.

AMONG AUTHORITIES AS WELL AS SUBORDINANTS.

WITH THIS REALTY IN MIND

Words of Inspiration

GOD HAS MADE PROVISIONS FOR ALL TO RECEIVE FORGIVENESS IN THEIR FAILINGS.

WHEN A LEADER FALLS?

LEVITICUS 4:22-26

July 17, 2011

John E. Harrison

BEGGING VERSUS BELIEVING

A COUPLE ANNOUNCED THAT THEIR CHILD WAS HAVING SEIZURES AND THE DOCTORS WERE WITHOUT INSIGHT AS TO THE CAUSE OR THE CURE OF THE CHILD'S CONDITION.

IN EARNEST EFFORT TO SEEK AND INVOKE DIVINE INTERVENTION THE COUPLE SAID, "WE ARE BEGGING GOD TO HEAL HER."

WHILE I UNDERSTAND THE CRY OF PARENTS WHO'S CHILD IS IN TROUBLE. I ALSO UNDERSTAND THAT GOD DOES NOT RESPOND TO PANIC, FEAR, AND TEARS OR EVEN EXPRESSED NEEDS ALONE; HE RESPONDS TO FAITH.

BEGGING IS AN ACT OF DESPERATION.

ASKING IS AN ACT OF FAITH.

JESUS SAID IN MATTHEW 21:22

"AND ALL THINGS, WHATSOEVER YE SHALL ASK IN PRAYER, BELIEVING, YE SHALL RECEIVE."

Words of Inspiration

THEREFORE, IF YOU HAVE A DESPERATE NEED DON'T PRAY A PRAYER OF DESPERATION; PRAY A PRAYER OF FAITH.

ASK, BELIEVE AND RECEIVE.

July 24, 2011

Words of Inspiration

TRUST HIS LOVE

TOO OFTEN WE ARE NOT FORTHCOMING AND COMPLETELY HONEST WITH OUR CONFESSIONS OF FAULTS AND FEELINGS WITH THE PEOPLE WE LOVE BECAUSE OF OUR UNCERTAINTY ABOUT HOW THEY WILL RESPOND; SO WE DEVELOP A PATTERN OF MAKING PARTIAL CONFESSIONS, MAKING MINI DISCLOSURES WITH INTRODUCTIONS OF TRUTH WITHOUT FOLLOW-THROUGH WITH THE WHOLE STORY.

WE DO THIS BECAUSE WE ARE AFRAID THAT IF WE ARE TOO HONEST IT WILL NOT BE ACCEPTED, FORGIVENESS WILL BE WITHHELD AND RELATIONSHIPS WILL BE DESTROYED.

COULD IT BE THAT WE APPROACH GOD WITH THE SAME MINDSET, MAKING PARTIAL CONFESSIONS OF THINGS IN OUR LIVES THAT HE IS ALREADY FULLY AWARE OF BECAUSE WE DON'T TRUST HIS LOVE?

John E. Harrison

1 JOHN 1:9 TELLS US "IF WE CONFESS OUR SINS, HE IS FAITHFUL AND JUST TO FORGIVE US OUR SINS, AND TO CLEANSE US FROM ALL UNRIGHTEOUSNESS."

GOD'S LOVE ALWAYS RESPONDS TO TRUE CONFESSION AND REPENTANCE WITH FORGIVENESS, CLEANSING, RECONCILIATION AND RESTORATION.

TRUST ME. GOD'S LOVE IS A LOVE THAT YOU CAN TRUST.

July 31, 2011

Words of Inspiration

YOUR VISION IS YOUR BLUEPRINT

WHEN THE DREAM YOU HAVE FOR YOUR LIFE BEGINS TO AMASS UNTO ITSELF ALL OF THE CHARACTERISTICS OF A NIGHTMARE...REMEMBER YOUR VISION AND USE IT AS A BLUEPRINT TO GUIDE YOU IN ITS TRANSFORMATION. IN OTHER WORDS,

YOUR VISION IS YOUR BLUEPRINT

August 6, 2011

John E. Harrison

Words of Inspiration

John E. Harrison

About the Author

Pastor John Harrison is the founder and Senior Pastor of House of Prayer Christian Church, Incorporated, in Columbus, Georgia. Married to the former Mae Helen Dixon, of Florence, South Carolina, he is the father of two sons, Arnold and Erik; and two daughters, Mya and Ameka, who have blessed him with twelve grand children: Jason, Toya, Gary, Alexia, Betty, Tashara, Erika, Mannie, Imani, Fabian, Lovely, and Jayne.

Life was hectic as the fifth of six children born to John (Willie) and Janie Harrison of Bennettsville, South Carolina. He attended Kollock Elementary School, and Eastside High School, both located in Bennettsville. Additional achievements include a Bachelor's degree, with Magna Cum Laude honors, and membership into the National Criminal Justice Honor Society, at Troy State University, Phenix City, Alabama.

Pastor Harrison is a retired army First Sergeant, of twenty-two years, and a veteran of the Vietnam War. Places of residence include, Kansas, Kentucky, Georgia, and Berlin Germany, where daughter Mya was born. Since retirement from the army, Pastor Harrison has worked closely with mentally challenged individuals. The first twelve years were spent working with severely emotionally disturbed children, ages four through high school. Currently, he is employed as a case manager, providing psychosocial rehabilitative services for adults diagnosed with a mental impairment. This work is an integral part of his overall ministry calling.

As Pastor of HOPCC, John has been blessed and touched by many lives. He feels privileged to mentor one of God's finest ministry teams including, lead minister, Dorothy Franklin, ministers Keith and Markella Lee, minister Yvonda Bolton (his Armor Bearer), and son-in-law, minister Donald R. Feagin.

All these journeys, from the farm in South Carolina, to the jungles of south east Asia, to the dusty trails of the sand hills of Fort Benning, Georgia, to the guarding of Rudolph Hess, at Spandau Prison, Berlin, Germany, and the pastoring of a church, who's heart is reflective of God's indwelling spirit, are memories Pastor Harrison will cherish forever. He would not alter any areas of his life if granted the power to do so.

May God bless the remaining journeys.

www.ingramcontent.com/pod-product-compliance
Lightning Source LLC
Chambersburg PA
CBHW070639300426
44111CB00013B/2166